A Season of Small Insanities

ANDREA PORTER is a member of the Joy of Six Poetry Ensemble that has performed in the UK and the USA. She has been published in a variety of poetry magazines in the UK, Canada and the USA. She received an Escalator Award in 2005 and an Arts Council grant in 2006. She is also a fiction writer and has had short stories published and has recently completed her first novel. Her pamphlet Bubble was adapted for BBC Radio 4 by the playwright Fraser Grace. She writes a blog, We Liked It but not Quite Enough (www.welikeditbutnotquiteenough.blogspot.com)

Also by Andrea Porter

PAMPHLET
Bubble (Flarestack Press)

COLLABORATIONS
Flirtations (Joy of Six Publications)
Evidence (Joy of Six Publications)
Package (Joy of Six CD. Apples & Snakes Soundblast and PBS
   recommendation)

A Season of Small Insanities

Andrea Porter

SALT

CAMBRIDGE

PUBLISHED BY SALT PUBLISHING
14a High Street, Fulbourn, Cambridge CB21 5DH United Kingdom

© Andrea Porter 2009

The right of Andrea Porter to be identified as the
author of this work has been asserted by her in accordance
with Section 77 of the Copyright, Designs and Patents Act 1988.

Salt Publishing 2009

Printed in Great Britain by
the MPG Books Group, Bodmin and King's Lynn

Typeset in Swift 9.5 / 13

ISBN 978 1 84471 509 1 paperback

Salt Publishing Ltd gratefully acknowledges
the financial assistance of Arts Council England

1 3 5 7 9 8 6 4 2

Contents

for my daughter

Acknowledgements

Acknowledgements are due to the editors of the following publications: *Boomerang, Canon's Mouth, Envoi, Ink Sweat and Tears, Nth Position, Red Lamp* (Australia & UK), *The Same* (USA), *Rattapallax* (USA), *The SHOp, Seam, Tempus* (Canada & UK). Some poems appeared in the following anthologies: *A Room to Live In* (Salt Publishing), *Blinking Eye Anthology* (Blinking Eye Press), *Forward Anthology of Modern Poetry 2005, The Gift* (Gatehouse Press).

A small selection of poems appeared in the pamphlet *Bubble* (Flarestack Press). The poems were subsequently adapted into a BBC Radio 4 play by the playwright Fraser Grace and broadcast in 2005.

A version of the poem 'North Sea Women' appeared in a multimedia piece created in collaboration with Jane Wingfield (Digital Artist), Mark Wingfield (Composer) and Sian Porter (Graphic Artist and Writer). This work was commissioned by the European Fund, Norwich City Council and The New Writing Partnership. It can be seen at www.DNAvigate.co.uk.

I also wish to thank all those unsung heroes, the poetry editors and publishers who have supported my work. I would also like to thank Helen Ivory, Andrew Motion, Ruth Padel and Jo Shapcott who have awarded me prizes in various competitions. Many of these published or award winning poems or revised versions of them are included in this collection.

I am grateful to the wonderful Arvon Foundation for giving me two bursaries so that I could attend their residential poetry courses. I would also like to thank The New Writing Partnership for an Escalator Award and the Arts Council for a grant.

I would also like to thank the poet Jacob Polley who encouraged me to put forward this collection for publication and gave me such valuable feedback on these poems.

Not least I would like to thank all my fellow members of Joy of Six (www.joyofsix.co.uk) and all those other poets and people who have provided friendship, support and wine along the way (they know who they are).

I   A Season of Small Insanities

Mystic

Long ago she shed her skin each summer,
pale parchments were left on floral sheets.
Only those with a gift could interpret these
as the end of days, the dark beginnings.
She wore stiff calamine lotion as a mask
that cracked and crazed with each smile.
She moves in darkness now, slips quietly
from shade to shade, whispers the mantra
of ancient numbers, all the factors of sixty.
She uses her power to block out the sun
so totally that she leaves white shadows
where she walks. She can eclipse patios.
She is becoming translucent, she reads
scorched earth, famine in her own entrails.

Laying On of Hands

The night before we stood on a hill overlooking Lourdes.
The procession unravelled, an ammonite of light.
They sang something involving 'Marias' and 'Aves',
words wove with The Beach Boys on the transistor.
Get around round round, I get around.
We both lay naked in your tent, the twisted boy
and the lanky girl trying too hard to fit together.
We stayed after every candle in the valley went out.
The hinge of your calliper was imprinted on my thigh.

Next day cutting through heat and light and wheelchairs
this boy-faced priest smiled. He put you in his shadow.
He had an accent, smelled of garlic and lemons.
He placed his quick hands upon your head, incanted,
then turned and reached up for mine. No eye contact.
You can fuck off wanker I thought you said.

We bought a plastic bottle shaped as the Virgin Mary,
filled it with holy water as a present for your Mum.
Later as we sat beside the coach park you fought
intention tremors to put your hand on my left breast.

Account of the Norwegian Antarctic Expedition

'The sun left us on April 22, and we did not see it again for four months'
— ROALD AMUNDSEN

This is another day for stillness.
I will sit quietly and conserve.
Cleaning the floor is too energetic,
that would demand more time
spent later in an icy shower.
Turning this page is manageable.
I will read Amundsen's account.
The trick to keeping cool is to see
Ole Engelstad's great snow cone
rise in the air to 19,000 feet,
and reach Lat. 86° 21′ south
at the foot of the Devil's Glacier.
After the journey when I look up
and see you, I will not burn.

Room

The distance gauged between the corner
of a coffee table and the curve of a sofa.
Our boundaries set by the furnishings,
are fixed by custom, until you bring
an old chair down from the attic.
It alters the map. Like the blind we explore
the edges, reshape a different interior.
We move more carefully for a while.

Eves

Adam insists he still needs Mother Eve
to complete dominion over the wasp.
Child Eve hurtles into autumn leaf piles,
smears apple jelly on her breasts and thighs.
Woman Eve shows herself to passing serpents
who flicker their tongues and coil around her.
Mother Eve drives home, tired and anxious.
She inspects Child Eve for signs of knowledge
while Woman Eve sips a cocktail on the terrace.
When Adam comes home, they knead his neck,
ease out the knotted day from his flesh. He sighs.
His shoulders recall that fired moment of becoming.
The Eves smile, they can see the power of one
but they understand the wisdom in numbers.

Traffic

The swallow at the base of his thumb flexes its wings.
Her right hand flutters to the strap of her scuffed bag,
inside; sunglasses for bruises, lipstick, a leather purse.
The purse is empty, except for a photograph she tore
from a magazine left in a drawer, of Johnny Depp.
That was fourteen weeks ago; she keeps him
behind the cellophane window made for family.

She has learnt some sayings now.
There are dogs and cats in rain, mouths full of frogs,
tears in fallen milk, a bird in his hand, socks to be pulled.

At the crowded junction he grasps her left hand.
She hesitates, looks up at the lights.
He says her name, is it Katya or Irena now?
The last vowel sound escapes from his mouth
as a quick pump of air, a tiny explosion.

They cross as the cars come to a stop on red.
Here traffic is obedient, compliant to the rules.

Visitors' Book
(Holiday Cottage Entry)

When coming down stairs
from the top floor
careful of last step.

Also watch out for mat near toilet—
likes to send you flying—
you need to get a grip.

A&E in Kendal—
nurses and doctors great.
Asda next door to hospital
do family meal—
£10—
very filling.

Sodom Cookery
(Genesis 19:26)

The skinny boy without front teeth
will come soon, take his dulled knife,
hack at my belly, take handfuls home
in his dirty sack to give to his mother.
She will salt beef strips for the winter.
Too much salt though can ruin them.

The wild ox licks my left thigh, he has
hollowed a valley down to my femur.
I shudder at each rough urgent stroke.
Ox tongue pickled in aged wine vinegar
with cracked peppercorns and herbs
made a cheap meal in these hard times.

I loved to cook, above all my own fat hens.
You must remember to baste chicken.
There is nothing worse than food ruined
through lack of care and sheer stupidity.
I only glanced back because I thought
I'd left the stew pot boiling on the fire.

DIY

The vibrator was to be a present for a friend.
She'd heard that excuse before, however
not a single facial piercing twitched.

She talked me through the pros and cons:
texture, variable speed, the length,
a facility for clitoral stimulation,

whether the capacity to glow in the dark
was *really* essential, but safer
than a bedside candle during power cuts.

We discussed inbuilt obsolescence.
Some women prefer the simple,
more straightforward kind: point and go.

She mentioned the unreliability
of complex wiring and attachments
and that frequent use could wear out parts.

She personally recommended
having flexibility to find your G-spot.
She advised against lending it to a friend.

There was a voice activated one
new on the market, you turn it on
by talking but they've had complaints.

Only shouting seems to make it work.
Thank you, I said, I'll take any one
that can laugh or whisper my name.

Sharp

In the drawer my bread knife has grown dull
through disuse, the edge is gone from the steel.
I always buy a wrapped, sliced loaf these days.
My father would clamp loaves firmly down
with his left hand and saw thin even slices
with his right. It was his role, like carving beef,
jointing a rabbit or taking the top off my egg.
I knew about cutting, that it was an art to hone,
like suitable comments around a joint of beef.
Any sharper and you'll cut yourself, young lady,
my mother would say. I learnt how to be silent.
Bread, meat, rabbit, egg; for each a particular knife.
The right tool for the right job, he would announce.
I watched, one day I would be trusted with knives.

Fighting the Bit

He hooks up the curb chain.
A 'martingale' stops the mare throwing her head.
A stargazer, you have to break her,
she must learn not to fight the bit.

She told me if you sing every verse
of 'Onward Christian Soldiers'
while you boil an egg it will be perfect;
white firm, yolk runny.

As her syphilitic fever rose,
Mrs Beeton whisked the egg whites
to stiff peaks. She whipped in
the air from her lungs, each lie.

I am not a ghost haunting
the Rutherford labs.
I didn't see them crack open an atom,
or catch the white of Shiva's eye.

No omelettes without breaking eggs
she writes in her letter. If I hold
it up to the light I can see the
stain of a yolk, a thread of blood.

On my night walks the moonlight
picks out the old battery hen sheds.
They are settling down into quiet decay,
even the rotted planks are muted.

In Saudi, imported Japanese swordsmen
separate a head from its neck, tender
in the completion of the task. It is neater
and faster, like slicing the top of an egg.

Every night she gazes into the sky,
skimming light from the dark like fat.
She can name the hunter, bear and belt.
Her head is thrown up and back.

Unstable Particles

A recuperative holiday with an English host can reduce the amount of
radioactive caesium which has built up in a child's body

The girl from Belarus lies inert in bed,
a new pink candy-striped duvet
twisted round her skinny body.
She wants to stroke her pale face.

She has taken down the old rosettes.
Second in the Obstacle Race.
Best under Ten Miniature Garden.
Does this thin child need a night light?

A child should not have to feel her way
through strange dark corridors
or trail her fingers along the walls,
to find where she needs to be.

This girl will grow, sit in a kitchen,
drinking tea with frail descendants.
Three weeks to feed her oranges.
Three weeks to host those eyes.

A whip of air from the window lifts
the corner of a faded Buffy poster.
This sleeping child holds out a half life,
part of the woman reacts and splits.

Venus and Cupid and a Man Playing a Lute
After Titian

I'm the porky toddler man,
handcuffs of fat clamped
around my ankles and wrists.
Genitals so tiny 'strumming boy'
there can hardly keep his face
straight as I heave into view.

No humming bird me
vibrating to a delicate F sharp.
My wings cut the air
with all the swoosh and stoop
of a hefty diving bird
spotting a juicy mackerel.

But she expects me to hover,
place this wreath of flowers
on her coiffeured head.
She wants me to fan her,
displace one tendril on her brow,
teased out for effect.

My down draught alone would
strip blooms from stalks.
Love that doesn't mess your hair
isn't worth a fucking arrow.

Orosia Moreno

After Goya's drawing of her appearance before the Inquisition

I am accused of the creation of mice.

From my body I have produced
these tiny creatures,
to piss in the confessional,
scrabble behind the skirting boards of priests,
interrupting prayers and rosaries,
robbing pale Fathers of sleep and consolation.

I have issued forth legions
from every orifice,
birthing them to infest pews,
terrify pious ladies in purple silks,
swarm over the altar cloth,
nibble and gnaw gold brocade
to holey rags,
form glittering nests to nurture young.

They have darted beneath habits of Jesuits
as they raised body and blood.
Drowned out bells with squeak and chatter,
bitten the balls of bishops and monsignors
as they slept on sheets stitched by sour nuns.

I have buried cathedrals in their droppings
and called each rodent child by their name,
Magdalene, Xavier, Torquemada,
Jesus, Pablo, Sebastian, Isabella.

They have scaled brass lecterns,
perched on open church bibles,
tails hanging like bookmarks across
numbered chapter and verse,
each printed office of the day.
At the end of days they shall judge

all onlookers, priests and kings.
Blessed are the mice,
for they shall inherit the earth.

Head

In 1888 Goya's body was exhumed in France, so that he could be buried in his native Spain. It was discovered that his head was missing. For the last thirty years of his life Goya was totally deaf.

I keep Goya's head under my bed.
I bring him out on Wednesdays
and buff the skull with a J-cloth dowsed in Pledge.
I thread it carefully through each socket
to ensure a perfect dust free finish.

I put the head on a red cushion. I cook paella
with organic rice I have discovered in Asda.
Sitting opposite, I offer him a Chilean wine.
He declines; he would prefer Rioja.

We talk for an hour or two about art,
lithography, the political situation in Spain.
I try to avoid the morality of bull fighting
as this usually leads to lengthy silences.

Then I tell him, Francisco, snap out of it.
Life is a bitch and then you're dead.
At least your head gets an outing.
El Greco has never seen The Bill or
a live transmission of the Turner Prize.

I know that he can hear me quite well,
death being a major cure for deafness.
It is hard to cajole him out of his moods.
The frustration at being separated
from his hands, now buried in Madrid,
makes him cry oily tears now and then.

Room Service

There are stains on the bottom sheet.
I never think now about their source,
just the residue of people I never meet.

I fret over the Do Not Disturb signs.
It will all need doing eventually;
beds, bins, towels, everything's mine

to arrange properly, tidy their mess
line up the sachets of shower gel,
clean the toilet, dust the trouser press.

They leave me clues from what remains,
what they do, what books they read,
whether they chew gum, those grains

of fine sand caught between their toes,
which I can identify from near the pier
or sand dunes by their texture. I know

more than they think. The wet patch
of tears on the pillow, the stale smell
of sex, the blonde hairs that match

those left by the woman in Room Ten
in her hairbrush, beside the photograph
of a tall man and two smiling children.

When he checks out he may leave a tip,
a fiver on the bedside table, I'll pocket it,
check the mirror for the seal on my lips.

Night Porter

This is a season of small insanities.
The hotel heaves with constant activity.
Guests arrive and check out without notice,
just a note propped on the bedside table.
One guest has changed from a double
to a single and then back to a double
in less time than it takes me to polish
the lobby, dust out my pigeon holes.
It rains continually and some guests
tap the barometer in hope of change.
I wipe their fingerprints from the glass.
Late at night I answer their calls for ice.

I check who wants waking with morning tea,
which newspaper they need to start the day.
I walk the corridors, eavesdrop at doors
for the sounds of laughter, sighs and weeping,
conversations, the click of a suitcase
being closed for another moonlight flit.
In my back room I tune in the radio
to the weather and a late night quiz show.
There are no questions that I can answer.
The front desk requires a new black biro.
Better during these strange times
to write in light pencil in the register.

North Sea Women

They arrive from the sea at night.
With every shot of tequila gold
they lick salt from their hands
to remind themselves of home.

Earlier they checked in wet coats,
promised the cloakroom boy a tip,
a real kiss, their mobile number,
if he'll keep them safe from harm.

Southern Comfort on the rocks
clinks against the sides of glasses,
they smile, sing under their breath.
A carpet fitter drowns in their eyes.

They dance close with fluid hips,
ebb and flow around their handbags
that open with a click like an oyster
to reveal coral-red lipstick, abalone combs.

They pass the jugglers and fire eaters
outside the clubs. They walk in shadows,
for fire is the ancient element; it makes
moist skin steam and boils their blood.

The late night tide of cars and taxis
closes over their heads, laughter
bounces off slow water. They wander
to the pier, ease into another life.

Night Shift at the Petrol Station

I

By four the fragile loners are drawn in,
attracted by the light. They drift and float,
press heads and hands against the glass,
their thin skin pale as milk veined wings.
They mumble about tobacco, chocolate,
bread, fag papers, the bright face of god.

II

The soft porn arrives in taped boxes.
Thrown from the van, it skids into
the pine smell of a newly mopped floor,
She unpacks it under buzzing strip lights.

Inside, fondled breasts, spread legs,
the razzle dazzle of flesh opened up.
It's her job to cover these women,
place every one in a 'modesty bag'.

There all night, behind bulletproof glass,
she's served drunks, stoned boys, police,
taxi drivers, bouncers, weary women
demanding nappies, aspirin and sleep.

She ticks off the list of things to be done;
line up bottles of cheap Chardonnay,
clean the toilets, re-stack mayonnaise,
write off all the past-their-sell-by-date.

This is her final job, the dawn censor,
sealing in, thighs, readers' wives, fake tans,
fingers placed to simulate masturbation,
moistened lips, thrusting tongues and hips.

Each one enclosed in their black plastic burqa,
their probing eyes peer out at every browser,
passerby, child. The top shelf women wait,
hint at what is hidden, watch her cash up.

Asleep at the Wheel

Bedded down in curtained cabs, parked
up near the crematorium entrance
on the A14, the lorry drivers dream of
naked women draped in cats' eye necklaces,
giant wildeyed rabbits braced for impact,
Mrs Driver's beef casserole and dumplings,
being buried alive in drifts of unclaimed ashes.

Zimbabwean Singer Detained in the Fenland Immigration Centre

I ask a guard about this long yellow singing in the fields;
so dazzling top note strong and it seems to go on for ever.

'Rape, it's called rape,' he says. Not a good word I think
for something so sunshine that syncopates this stretch.

I have seen this word, its shadow in soldiers' eyes,
heard it howling out a dark crop in women's lives.

I would not give it this name but who am I to choose
the words to use for this land. At home I would welcome

someone passing my grandfather's fields, a tired boy
trudging past, who stops to admire its fierce gold.

Come, look at our 'bright singing', here they say rape;
here no one glories in the colour of common things.

Postcard From Jerusalem

I have sent the Wailing Wall to Mrs Payne.
Yesterday I wandered with the tour group
as they snapped, swam with the heat haze
before holy sights. They clung to bum bags,
lifebelt passports and traveller cheques.
I was drawn to the old rituals of the Wall,
the rocking, the forehead touch, the kiss.
An American scrubbed with wet wipes
before the act. Tiny scrolls of prayers
filled every slim crack as paper mortar.

I flattened my breasts to the stone, my lips
brushed the grain and touched the scars.
I tasted the sour dust of falling homes,
petrol fumes from a packed rush hour bus,
the bitter stench of sweat and smoke.
I pushed my tongue deep into the open
fissures. The tip reached the salt.
Deeper in were settlements with gods,
tube maps. Blue prints of bunkers fizzed
in my mouth like bitten sherbet lemons.

I explored each crevice, found meaty truths
snagged between the wisdom teeth of Pilate.
I gagged on incense, the thick sugar-coat
of words. I licked the stamp for her card,
left the Wall in the gum and posted it home.

Heike with her Dictionaries

Alone in a small commercial hotel you summon other thoughts,
tell yourself the shower curtain is the colour of a silk scarf
you bought in Dublin last November, drink lukewarm herbal tea
from a mug you have carried with you since Kiev,
remember rice on a patterned plate in Cambridge,
how the weight of technical dictionaries strained
your back on the train home from Frankfurt airport.
The tiny buff tag on the tea bag catches you out.

Numbering evidence from Bosnia.
Sixteen days of written statements
made to a commission in The Hague.
Four days of photographs.
Forensic. Focused. No faces.
A metre stick laid beside a trench gave a sense of scale.

Buff cardboard tags on body parts.
Tissue samples. Skulls. Bones.
Catalogued. Identity unknown.
Shown neat rowed to the lens.
Rewind.

J five stroke seven four nine.
M eight oblique three two one.
Translate the numbers. Never stumble over one.
Pour from one jug of language to another.
Never lose a single drop of blood.
Never stop to open flood gates to unprofessional emotion.
Justice requires precision.

Life is in the detail. Death is in the detail.

Fast forward. Fast fast forward.

Summered forest floor green flushed with nettles.

Echolalia of meaning in your head, different taste in your mouth.

They brought six soldiers here. They dragged six boys here.
They executed them here. They shot them here.
Gesture left to speak.
They buried them here. They hid them here.
Gesture left to speak.
Pause. Rewind. Play Kosovo.

Mrs Stenman on her Newspaper House in Pigeon Cove, Massachusetts

It kept us all busy, a family with purpose,
each evening, backwater weekends
rolling the news up; creating furniture,
walls, using tight tubes to make shelves.

The newsprint would stain our hands.
Each hour of twist, stick and lacquer
left us blackened. Events were printed
on our palms, a reverse of the times.

A clock, a piano, a bookcase, chairs;
made from storms, local flower shows,
Scopes Monkey Trial. A fallen bankrupt
is a mantelpiece for our photograph.

I confess we cheated on the piano,
we covered only the exterior walnut.
Newspapers are notoriously silent
only a rustle, scrunch or crumple,

the thwack of a blow to the body
maybe but no hope of a single note,
let alone Maple Leaf Rag or Beethoven.
Elis brooded over paper keys.

We handled Lindbergh's flight for weeks,
Celebrity, hero, world and breaking
inked onto every finger, until our hands
were coated in a film of admiration.

The desk was a tribute and a triumph.
The varnish darkened each year
as other headlines rolled; kidnap, eugenics,
Anti-Semitism. No news about the war.

Azrael Visits The Angel Shop In Edinburgh

I stood at the gates of Eden,
warming myself at the sword.
I watched Lucifer topple
from the edge of glory.

I have shattered cosmic laws.
Ripped fabrics of consequence,
holding worlds by one thread,
dowsing for their redemption.

I have roamed their dreams,
wrestled them, taken first born,
demanded belief beyond sanity,
proclaimed the loss of reason.

Now with this burning quill
plucked from my left wing,
I have written their names,
all those who come to shop.

Let them try to move a mouse
over me, drink from my image,
pin me to a polyester dress
or display me as an ornament.

My sigh can shake high towers.
Wonder does not cost £8.99,
it cannot be found in tea towels.
Awe will not be sent as a text.

The Last Vertigo

They were angels once, the beat of wings
turned to crank, their backbone to pivot.
They throb, tethered to this last height
before sea level, naked in their revolution.

A fen underlines the erect stance of the tall.
They tease the last sun in from the taut
horizon. They wheeze, wind slowly and form
a skein of light into a thick three-ply moon.

The air pushes at their pale sculpted arms,
a flick of a wrist and a sigh from the east
is scooped up, transformed to power;
a drove, gaudy with lumens and candela.

As I stand and watch them, I recall falling;
flailing the dark like them, unable to cling
to the last dream of wonder. This ground
reminds me of how sudden descent can be.

As I look up, my new found vertigo spins,
and my leg muscles judder in the engine
of flight or fight. The memory of breaking
pushes up through my long femur shaft.

We rooted tall structures know each other,
fallen is written through us, end to end,
sucked down to *all*. We know flat, the fear
of unbroken horizons, of never rising again.

Assassinations

JOHN F. KENNEDY *d.*1963

I was sitting crosslegged in my grey school skirt
in front of Josie Hibbert's tiny Bakelite TV.
Upstairs her Mum was dying of something quiet.
We ran upstairs to tell her and she cried.

MARTIN LUTHER KING *d.*1968

I was with a black haired boy called Dave,
in his room still decorated with Noddy wallpaper.
Downstairs his Mum cooked egg and chips
in a long sleeved blouse to hide the bruises.

STEPHEN BANTU BIKO *d.*1977

I was walking through the Arndale Centre.
A TV called to me from a shop window.
Two stores up a shabby man was shouting.
Security was there telling him to move on.

JOHN LENNON *d.*1980

I was sitting at a green Formica table.
Across from me a girl was smoking roll ups.
She'd gouged zigzags into both her arms.
We drank tea as she picked at the scabs.

Boxes

I have thirty-four heart-shaped boxes;
maple, yew, jade, silver and onyx.
Each is beautiful but they have a purpose;
they hold secrets, keep things contained

This one in marble was bought in Riga,
a woman at the roadside held it out.
I liked the look and feel of it,
cooler than the heat of my hand.

The one there, with the pearl inlay lid,
was a present from my father's friend.
Look closely, it has a slight lilac tinge.
At twelve I knew the power of keys.

I have to move them to clean underneath.
I catch up with the house on a Thursday.
They like things to be nice,
fresh towels, flowers, polished handcuffs.

Three Haiku for a Saint

Found statue, a burnt branch of a willow struck by lightning,
Kettles Yard, entitled Saint Edmund *by Jim Ede*

seed becomes the tree
bowed to the insistent course
bent backed to heaven

a spark to the heart
the fierce act of creation
fired to glorify

fleshed by each dark step
the skin crazed as one branded
by nature to burn

Man Insults Veiled Medusa on the Tube

Cobra, Anaconda, Vine,
Rainbow, Rosy-Boa, Ground,
Speckled, Copperhead and Spit.

All of these you call only snake.

Royal Python, Chain-King, Corn.
Carpet, Pigmy, Milk and Grass
Coachwhip, Racer, Ringneck, Night.

See a myth of slime and slither.

Mountain, Water, Temple, Pine.
Mangrove, Glossy, Diamondback.
Dawn-Blind, Sunbeam, Pipe and Dice.

Miss every complex dovetailed scale.

Common, Leopard, Wolf and Tree
Black-Rat, Scarlet, Viper, Reed,
Rough-Earth, Tiger, Dusky, Queen.

Hands Free

I calculate every minute in rent and council tax.
I am skilled at hearing without ever listening,
respond but do not engage. I have talent
and now I have bought a hands-free phone
I can pant as I iron tea towels and sheets,
moan during a silent video of *Pretty Woman*.

I promise myself that when my numbers come up
or when my great aunt in that big house in Cromer
has that final stroke, I will put the phone down,
yank out the plug and throw it out of the window.
No more lies about underwear, as I pick melted
chocolate from my jeans or read *Madame Bovary*.

I am adept at lip reading but subtitled DVDs
are more convenient. *La Haine*, *Wings of Desire*
are less intrusive as a man on a bad mobile line
suggests I pleasure myself with a wine bottle.
Regulars ask for me by a name at the call centre,
I chose Anna, a woman who died in a Tolstoy story.

They like her, appreciate all Anna's art and craft.
They say thank you, some ask how she's keeping
after business is done. Now and then I hang up
on those who abuse her, bruise without touch.
As for the rest, she can sell a credit card whore
formed from dirt words, a polished rib of my voice.

American Carnie Freaks, 1902

The flyer lists Irena 'The Giantess',
as presented at the court of the Czar.
A novelty between Faberge eggs,
sickly Siberian tigers bound for a zoo,
the latest treat for a bleeding child.
More probably a daughter of immigrants,
her young head already poking above
the crush of Ellis Island hopefuls.

She'd have grown beyond usefulness
on a farm, or taken up too much space
in a crowded New York tenement.
Given, found, abandoned or bought.
There is something of the laudanum
in the look she gives to the camera.
She is already beginning to stoop
under the weight of curious eyes.

Perhaps she needed something for pain,
something to dull the everyday viewing
by shuffling lines of Iowa farmhands,
bored shop workers from Minnesota.
She is dressed in a creased ball gown,
posed between two male dwarves
who stretch up to hold her hands.
They both look up in staged adoration.

The touch, how her fingers were held,
could never be captured by the lens.
On telegraph poles leading into towns,
in the windows of cluttered general stores
she is the current attraction, along with
the strongman, seal boy, a two-headed ram.
She is worth far less than Siamese twins,
and could be traded for a bearded lady.

Shaman

For Siân

From the time she could hold a spoon
she collected broken things.
Toys unsold at jumble sales
were retrieved from waste bins;
abandoned items lessened by malice
or wrecked by careless others.

The grubby bear without eyes,
his stitched mouth unravelled to silence.
The Barbie, feet chewed by terriers,
her skin scarred by red felt pen.
The baby doll that jutted from a skip
at the headfirst angle of abandon.

She accepted each as they were.
She bound immediate wounds,
sat them on every surface or
crowded them into her narrow bed.
She arranged them in family groups,
with no connection, other than a history.

She created their stories in her head,
recited them to all who would listen.
She incanted rites of bonding; older,
more powerful than plastic moulding.
She celebrated all acts of damage,
made each injury a sign of power.

The naked scalp of Sindy was tattooed
with intricate crimson runic symbols.
She wrapped strips of sequined ribbon
around the burst belly of an elephant.
The bear was given a dragon's fire tongue.
Dolls had empty sleeves stitched with pearls.

At night when air slowed to the pace of a frost,
she lay in her bed surrounded by survivors.
She sang them tunes from *My Fair Lady*,
humming the forgotten or unknown words.
She glorified the silence, in the company
of all those she had chosen to keep.

Heart FM

He described the sound of his heart
on the long drive back from hospital.
That time it was moths trapped in a jar.
Later there was; studded boots on attic floors,
a leaf shudder in high winds, a prosaic thud,
a collision of flour sacks, shrugs in an anorak,
a heavy suitcase dropped on a platform.
He listened to his heart, preset to the frequency.

It was an old family story that my father
had driven them all mad during the war,
constantly fiddling with the radio,
trying to get a perfect reception.
Screeching seared their ears. Up and down,
up and down the dial every night,
searching for the location of clear news.
Dunkirk, Coventry, D-Day, Hiroshima.

Now he was always finely tuned.
His skeleton was a vibrating cat's whisker,
his grey eyes hot crystals.
The rib cage caught waves and amplified,
the skull became a bony speaker.
He was his own private receiver.
That last Tuesday, he sat propped up;
the oxygen mask, a jaunty party hat.

How is it today? *The sea at Skegness pier.*
In four years he had remained precise.
As I bent to kiss him I wondered
what the last sound would be;
a minute's radio silence for the fallen,
a short break between programmes,
a brief hiccup in the schedule,
white noise.

Plane Ride

My mother heard Glen Miller
broadcast live on the radio
just before he disappeared.
She danced to 'String of Pearls',
'In the Mood', 'Moonlight Serenade',
with a Canadian navigator
she had invited home to tea.
They waltzed and circled the table,
her mother's best china,
the remains of a seed cake.

She remembers he went missing
in action, his pale blue eyes,
that he came from Manitoba
but not where she lives
or that her husband has died.
She twirls on in that Mecca,
but she sits out a quick step,
tells me that planes are risky.
You never come back from
some flights or journeys.

Picking Things Over

Each Friday I buy frozen North Atlantic prawns.
I leave them to defrost on my draining board
until their whiskers begin to tremble once more
and their raised full stop eyes shine from the sieve.
I present them to her in a small plastic bag
and we enact our usual piece of theatre.
Fresh prawns, she says, opening the bag.
You can still smell the sea in them. Remember
all those good holidays we had in Skegness,
those prawns from the stall near the floral clock?

There, head bent over an enamel bowl, she picked
them clean. She kept them cool in the freezing brine
I dredged from the North Sea in my plastic bucket.
I scuffed at the water's edge. Behind me, Dad dozed,
then gave up and went for a pint. My brother sulked,
asked for money for the penny arcades or crazy golf.
I grew dizzy as I gazed down at all the ebb and flow.
Now I watch her slowed hands fight to release
each prawn, empty husks heaping up on newspaper.
We can both smell the deceit, the salt of it all.

Continuity Girl

Midday, you find her asleep in another rehearsal.
Her mouth gapes, falls open into a weighted rest.
Her chest barely rises, as you bend to the hush.
Your right cheek feels nothing, no kiss of air.
You watch yourself as her best handbag mirror,
is cupped in your palm and held to her mouth.
A breath is captured as its own softened image,
like a gauzy photograph of Miss Veronica Lake.
You examine the reflection for her remains then
straighten the sheets. You smooth her pillowcase,
brush the biscuit crumbs from her bedside table
and adjust all the props to maintain the illusion
that time has not passed. You check every detail
then consider not letting her walk back on the set.

Spindleruv Mlyn Bus Station

I placed my bag on the pale slush,
avoiding oil patches left by buses
going to all those destinations
I had practiced saying days before.

My stiff neck cracked as I looked up
at the sheaf of grey mountains, tied
with wide strips of December snow.
I realised you were no longer there.

You did not wonder where you were.
I would not be needed to change
incontinence pads, tell you names
and places or sit and brush your hair.

The woman in the caged ticket office
had patted my gloved hand through bars,
told me, *Other buses to Praha come,*
wait and you will be delivered ok. OK

The bus was late, I waited into night,
I waited as streets tipped into neon.
Delivery did arrive, it slid up to me
as I tried to keep upright on the ice.

'Pray for Our Hometown Heroes in Iraq'

We make it to the statue of Johnny Appleseed
before your need for a Marlboro and sweet coffee
slips into the Toyota with the airconditioning.
Further on, down the Mohawk Trail in Templeton,
we stare at the sign in the convenience store.
Four photographs of boy-men, a felt tipped notice.
These could be our sons, scrubbed and smiling,
if we had borne those sons that could go to war.
Next door 'The Ice Cream Barn', melts in the heat,
vanilla paint dribbling down the clapperboard.
They would have eaten every flavour here,
Saturday after Saturday, until nothing was left
to taste except this leaving of worn benches
and the red neon air above the Coke machine.

At Emily Dickinson's Grave
Born December 10th 1830. Called back May 15th 1886

It is written here in stone that Emily was called back.
She wasn't put on hold, she didn't find the line busy.
Whilst waiting for this call she used her time well;
she wrote, made it down those four steep steps
from her door in icy winters to walk to the church.
She sat on her porch in spring, arranging small twigs
from the oak into fifty-five interesting hyphens.
She addressed letters in her best handwriting.
She never went far from home, the call could come
and she might have been in The Moan and Dove
or eating in the Paradise of India on Main Street.
Now she's got the numbers of those who leave
their business cards or letters on her headstone.
She'll call back, when she's ready or has the time.

Yield

The drivers on New York arteries are blooded
by the necessity of cut and thrust, but holding
our ground is something we know how to do.
We rant in unison at those that fail to read
the signs. You shun your horn, unlike some,
who play the two-tone shuffle through the toll.
We get the lone finger, the mimed arsehole
from New Jersey plates, he reads windscreens,
faces, he sees our future in a muscle twitch.
Don't they understand what bloody yield means?
No answer is required but it settles on the car
with the puddle dirt, the billboard shadows.
I keep trying to master the art of this verb,
how to read it, the road behind us and ahead.

II   Marrying Richard Harris

Clockwork

One act omitted or committed
and you could miss each other
in the dark or catch only headlights
glaring in the rear view mirror.
One person has to stop for a piss,
another insists on fish and chips,
the third drinks a seventh scotch.

It's as if you are consulting watches,
adjusting, comparing, fiddling
with the second hand to ensure
everything remains on schedule.
External factors are arranged perfectly.
The traffic lights are the correct sequence,
a puddle is formed and frozen,
an elm was planted eighty years before.

Chat

The weather, Leeds United's need to find a decent striker,
your cousin's party, did you remember to leave out the
tins of cat food for Beattie to find, will she remember to
feed him, are the couple at number sixteen feeding him
anyway, how much you love him, is Mr. Green's bypass
working, has somebody gone for help, will the pipes be
frozen when you get home, that last surgeon's exam you
have to take, is Barry having it off with that staff nurse,
the sash window you still have to mend, what time it is,
should you paint the kitchen, tomorrow, how cold it is.

Snow Night

You are talking about hot tea when he dies,
hear him stop breathing, become silenced.
So quiet this snow on early hour streets.

You take his next breath and the next
and the next as if you can fill his still body
by sympathetic magic, numbered acts of will.

You breathe, even when noise drowns you,
air becomes liquid with sirens and voices,
flooding, bursting through each strained lung.

You feel for the sternum, resting your hand
on that same place that is the night familiar
to winter lovers who sleep folded together.

The rise does not come but you can sense
the pulse in your own thumb, name it as his
and lift the bone to make a canopy for a beat.

You watch his lips, taste them cooling to slate,
but believe you can tongue the poisoned apple
from his mouth and wake him with slow kisses.

Handling

The hospital trolley has a wonky wheel,
corners badly, makes a strange noise
every revolution. It needs expert handling.

This porter has a knack of heading
at oblique tangents to his destination
to achieve all the required results.

Doorways come at you from odd angles;
head, feet, never quite parallel to walls.
The cellular blanket is slipping to the left.

You hug your belly tight to your spine.
It still appears in control, even possible, then
he hits a drip-stand and you smell the petrol.

Elegy

His liver weighs in at just over a kilo.
That last cup of cheap Co-op coffee
dribbles across the stainless steel pan.

The stomach is still distended
from that late stop at the chippie.
The batter is partially digested.

The lungs, each sac expelled of air
drawn from a lover's mouth,
are eased into formaldehyde.

Pinning back bruised skin
other organs are readily available.
The skeleton does not protect the bowels.

All the genitalia; penis, testicles, scrotum
have their state dictated;
each comma and full stop specified.

The heart is excised, the scalpel
relieves it of loose connections.
It is lifted whole, deficiencies still bloody.

Last there is the Black & Decker entry
through the skull, a clockwise rotation.
Hemispheres are manouvered out of bone.

Slivers are placed onto slides,
the microscope adjusted for clarity.
Every specimen is fixed.

These will be filed for reference,
should there be a reason
to examine a particular grief.

Black Hole

Contractions are just that,
the sense that your body
is imploding, falling in
on itself, trying to become
a small fist of darkness,
heavy with the gravity of pain.
It spins somewhere between
your lower spine and navel,
pulling in energy, mind, nurses,
drips, doctors, rubber gloves,
forceps, heart monitors and light.

Altered State

When you're shown your child
still bloody from the journey,
something changes,
something changes.
When you're shown the second
nothing changes,
nothing changes.
The alchemy has happened,
the transformation made.
Love from love,
life from the dead,
the glittering prize
from a lump of lead.

Double Act

The blue sister tells you one is always the stronger.
What was it he called them, his hands on your belly,
Abbott and Costello, Laurel and Hardy,
Flanagan and Allen, Pete and Dud?

Which one are you, straight man or clown?
Who gives up the act first, puts the microphone down
nods to the crowd and makes for the wings?
There is one who appears to know how it's done

and the other takes life for just what it isn't.
He found banana skins strewn at the neck of the womb,
skidded into a tiled room and laughed at his entrance,
the swearing, flushed mother, the masked men and women.

Pointless to speculate when both are struggling
to stay on in this business. You will them on to perform,
become the great stand-ups whose timing is perfect.
You tell them you'll jump to your feet and applaud.

You promise over and over that you will get the joke.

Marrying Richard Harris

This was not what you wrote in your diary
when you were twelve years old.
Not this holding of a second dead child
in a room next to the scrape of plates,
all those uneaten fish Friday lunches,
the drumming of pipes in a busy sluice.

I will marry Richard Harris.
Sing on Top of the Pops.
Not bite my nails.
Fill a country house with children.
Write a book. Have pierced ears.
Drive a car.
Live in Ireland by the sea.
Wear jeans all the time.
Adopt stray cats and orphans.
Own two wolfhounds.
Ride a horse better than Christine White's.
Travel to one name from each page in my atlas.

This was the hope list in HB pencil,
your future plans in neat joined-up writing.
You rock him and cry as is called for.
Marrying Richard Harris would have avoided this,
stopped this falling apart
in a space set aside for the purpose.

Life Boats

This nurse is full of shit.
Grateful for small mercies.
Time is a great healer.
Worse things happen at sea.

You are thinking, you are thinking,
the boat is sinking.
Crew struggling with elements
too savage to endure.
Lying, lying too low in the water,
dragged now by an anchor
that once held fast.
When the bulkheads go
it will all be swept away
lost to tides and undertow.
And the ship, the ship
can run aground,
lie there for the wreckers,
but who will sew up
the sailors' shrouds,
put the last stitch through
specks of gristle nose
to confirm an end to pain?
Are worse things happening at sea?
Show me, show me now,
I've earned the right to see.

Home Help

She'd taken their cots apart,
stacked them in the shed,
stored baby clothes under
a neighbour's double bed.
Medical books are all hidden,
clothes to the Sally Army.
She thought it for the best,
cause you less distress.
She didn't want you sobbing
at diagrams he learned by rote
or a scruffy navy duffel coat.
She would have taken the air
in the kitchen away, carefully
scrubbed it clean of Sundays.
She overlooked the deep dip
in the mattress, failed to fill it.
Something to roll down into,
one thing left to cling to.

Caskets

He hands you a small display board,
sample rectangles in ordered rows.
Dark oak, light oak, deep mahogany,
rich rosewood, simple polished pine,
veneered walnut like a loved piano.
Hand-written labels on yellowing paper,
sellotape beginning to peel at the edges.

Service

You see mud on the hem of his surplice,
his nose is pink from the cold or a cold,
the word baby does seem adenoidal.
He's tried to clean his slip-on shoes
but there's clay packed in the ridges,
where the black uppers meet the soles.
Has he strode across ploughed fields,
honking into a monogrammed hankie?
Did he cut through the allotments?
He may have tramped in the turned soil
over there by the moss covered angel,
to be here again, on time, with his bible.

Second Hand

It's all in this booklet
about grief
and mourning,
the stages to expect.

Beattie gave it you
but it wasn't new,
it had been used before
by someone else.

The corner is turned down
on page fourteen,
there's a tea stain
in the right hand margin.

You unfold the crease
with trembling fingers,
read in the act that pain
never comes second-hand.

Registering

It must have been what you did yesterday.
Three death certificates behind the clock
with the red water rates you have to pay.
Beattie from next door says it's the shock
and offers you another fruit scone. It may
have been someone else? Who? Mental block
is so common these days. Will this all stay
unmarked? Such an important thing locked
up, locked in, the specific key hidden away.
Will you find it years later? Bite your lip, rock
back and forth in front of strangers, replay
it when you see a paisley maternity smock?
Can that grey man reaching for a pen that lay
just to his left be forgotten or just held at bay?

No Returns

Those pads to soak it up cost too much
so you thrust thick wedges of loo roll
down your bra and end up peeling tissue
from your nipples in graffitied toilets

Debbie is a slag.
Linda is a cock sucker
Barry does it up your arse
Sandra loves Pete.

You stand in line in an anywhere Mothercare
to return nappies still in the cellophane.

No you've lost the receipts.
Yes it was a cash transaction
Yes, less than six weeks ago
No, in-store credit isn't any use to me.

You feel your T-shirt becoming sodden,
catch the eye of a horrified Saturday girl
who will rewind the image on the 37 bus
and replay it as a form of contraception.
Looking down you expect not a puddle,
but a river in spate, bursting crowded banks,
hurling prams, wipe-clean blue high chairs
into trees to dangle as twisted mobiles.

Crossing

When all this is over, snapped cables twisted
into the hollow of a river bed and rivets rusted
to crisp orange snow, there will be no one
to stride towards you with a lopsided smile.
There will be no hands thrust into pockets
or the ghosts of breath to drift and mingle
over guardrails. No wind will hum in girders
or whip strands of brown hair across a face.

When all this is over, a heart will not lurch
like a taxi cab and the fare will not be paid
in hoarded coins held back from gas meters.
The journey there will never seem endless.
The driver will not tell you over his shoulder
about the others who have been here before.